Monday's Letter

Smoove Babii

Presentation by *BookLeaf Publishing*

Web: www.bookleafpub.com

E-mail: info@bookleafpub.com

ISBN: 9789358736212

First edition 2023

This is to my guardian angel and I know you don't like the spotlight but you deserve this. Without you, this book and anything after this won't be possible! I thank you and love you, Ashley!

ACKNOWLEDGEMENT

I want to acknowledge every single person who has supported me in any kind of way! Whether it's coming to a show, reposting a video, buying my first book Ghetto Gospel, buying any type of merchandise, or just simply giving me feedback on a new piece! I thank you and love you!

Dear Pain

You motherf***er you! I'm so sick and tired of you. You always trying to mess up my inner mood. Always have someone in their Bourbon bag, that's how you hold the emotion in you. Wish I got throw hands with you. Toe tag and zip the bag up on you. I hate you! If you were a person man, I'll spit on you. I can't stand you because you only come around to take my people. Come on, you think you can just do what you want to do? Making look like a fool but I got a plan to deal with you. I keep escape routes. Dark or light whichever one is compatible. It feels good to put you right in the mood but then I feel all the blue. But I noticed ain't no getting away for you. You're around everything that I do so here's me saying bye from the guy who's FEARS you!

Monday's Letter

Dear Sex

You're something amazing. Something I can erase my head in, twist in, and have your body shapeshift. Clock in for the timing, have a brother change shifts. But you love to time it, while you climb it, ride it, hold it, then usher me to trading places. Turn my life over to god, have faith in, spread your legs for the saving, but you give in. Pipe dreams how different your world is with me. Are you kidding me, mind as well let me lick like we going half on a baby. Toes dancing like a routine got me doing magic mic moves. Just so I can prove I'm more than waist for you. I can love you but you skipped me in line.

Monday's Letter

By Smoove Babii

Dear Pen

I need your help to find another way to bleed besides laying in the streets from lead that doesn't come from a brother or the police. I'm trying to paint my own story while making history by telling my story without any stories! I need you to save me! If I don't turn to you, I'll in up in the pin acting out from anger that's birth within. My best friend's life came to an end and now I'm that dangerous friend. I'm ready to pass lives on sheets even if your ink runs out on me. 11/28/2010 is what changed me. A Song for Mamma turned me from a boy to a man. Your ink is saving me.

Monday's Letter

Dear Me

Everything is based on a meme and this is how it's supposed to but who knows me? Hell, I don't even know me. But I do know how to cover up what god's hands have arranged for me with some fake beauty or to conceal the truth about hands being put on me! See it's always something that makes me feel ugly so I do things to feel that inner sexy. I black out anytime someone whispers to me, boy I wish they would stay away from me. Matter of fact watch these thoughts breezy into a cool dream as I finally find someone who fits me. So as I slept, the last voice I heard was me. Signed the only person who tried to protect ME!

Monday's Letter

Dear Revenge

You're sweet, just like the lips on me. I see why Shorty was on me. She wanted me to lick her split but I told her, only if she's wifey!... But Shorty's game was tight, I can't even lie. From how preached, to the way her tongue had me weak. Man, I thought I finally found a blessing. So I started showing affection. But that quickly turned into a message. MESSAGE! Lil Mamma had me stressing. Her commitment was being tested. But I ignored the signs and gave her everything I was blessed with. Willing to deal with all her imperfections. Just took it little by little, you know in different sessions. Try to teach her how to step in but all she did was sleep in. Gave my bank account a recession. Had the inner me regressing. Man, she was an infection that gave infections! Had to put her ass on blast for a clap back session. Got burnt free, moved on, and started worrying about me. Three years later, I'm expecting my first baby engaged to the woman of my dreams. And as for her, heard she hasn't spoken to her best friend in three years!

Monday's Letter

Dear Eyes

There is something different about you today. I get the feeling that I'll be swimming against your waves. Let's follow the light through the tunnel because these emotions are weighing on your chest. I want you to just breathe. Put air back into your heartbeat despite those dark scenes you've seen. It's starting to reflect on your body of sea and all I see are C, average when it comes to reading energy. Your eyes are the most powerful thing on your body because it's not able to play Hide N Seek. You can put on a smile but your lens tells me that you are living inside of the abyss. When your waves collide against your face it causes it to change. I'm continuing to swim, to see what Cupid shot you with.

Monday's Letter

Dear Love

Why it's so hard for you to commit? Why do you have to pretend? Why can't you just let me in? I care for you like I'm the only one for you. I want to help you be a better you. I don't want to control you. I'm just trying to hold you. I want to give myself all to you. I want you to give me an out-of-this-world experience. So I can be experienced. Take you out the hood but keep the hood in you. Grow with you, get old with you, and install some trust in you. Lay with you. Bring the crown that goes on top of you because who doesn't want to be shot with a dose of you?

Monday's Letter

Dear Emotions

I know your present is in all of us but shy away from us men! Just wondering why it's so hard to let women in. I mean they only know when we regret. Don't know how to express myself without being called too SENSITIVITIE! Wearing you on our sleeves would be considered the wrong outfit. Mistreat is the outlet. Love like last week is a process. I'm trying to reverse that process. Like, stop treating your lips like it's a contest. Stop holding women's hearts like a hostage. Make change together, that's a profit. Put a ring on it, no options. Going through pain together, healing topics. Still, chase after her like she's your top pick. Don't make her a trending topic. Don't walk on her feelings like a carpet. Don't aim at her past like a target. Blow her head with your mindset and recreate the sound bites.

Monday's Letter

Dear Freedom

Can we talk freely about how free is a fee? You have to give something up to feel free. My thoughts can't wander because they don't like free-thinkers so me doing poetry is how I let my freedom ring. So to free write is for free rights but it still costs a fee once they throw the book at me. We have a right to feel free but our rights were never free. Had representation to try to keep me free but that was free so their "hard work" didn't come with a fee so why the hell would they fight hard to make sure I stay free? I look free but in reality, I'm a fee so they cage me to tame me and that's how they free-load off of me. I'm not even allowed to be free with my mental instabilities, the postpartum depression is killing me. I hear voices in my head that need to be free but the fee that I feed was the child that gained their wings! So what is free in life when life is nothing but fees?

Monday's Letter

Dear Rose

I had no idea you could be so cold. My heart ended up in the ICU but I saw you when you gave up on our love. So I allowed myself to just fade away in the darkness of empathy. I circled back to take an L as Venus's eternity. The goddess of love which I lost at sea rocking my boat as the ice came crashing down on me. I wrist it all by biting the hand that feeds. You saved me from the lock with your master key. I watched the band play as the water filled up inside of me. I watched you swim away blowing the whistle but never thought about saving me. You throw away the gem as a symbol of our freedom. You did that on our anniversary. Leaving petals on my ghetto concrete!

Monday's Letter

Dear Lost Keys

You got a nigga feeling incomplete. My whole life is on a couple of rings, my phone doesn't ring but you're outta range. They said you can be replaced but the feeling ain't the same. We got chemistry. You helped me get home safe even in my drunk rage. Put the key in the lock to unlock the safe but to keep things safe, I lock it back inside the safe. You worry me, you roam around the city with no security. Metal Across the Grain has similar body fame but the headspace is new to me. You were my galaxy, my shooting star that flew right by me but this mercury ain't healthy for me. You were my third rock from the sun, you can shine the light on me. I stroked your keys like Steven Wonder when he couldn't see the potency in my pen when I wrote this 4-page letter covering the left eye like that boy at the end of the road on a bending knee. God came down to get me. He hugged me. Sent Cupid right behind me to double eye me not why me, babii it's eazy. Use the teeth, I mad I lost this masterpiece! Can't no artist help recreate this identity? Don't box me, smile when you address me. Or I leave you hanging on the side, dry like a quickie. Quickly things can interrupt unlocking different characteristics to come out of me, split me like mental instabilities! The ability to write in my body CC me when you forward it to me, copy! I talk beyond the surface I get deep. 6 feet! I worship the ground above me, I see you open up Seas like O in the middle of me. Moses parted the Red Sea. I see red when it triggers my anxiety. I'm mad I lost the beat to the keys. I wear my emotions on my sleeve like a long sleeve. I aim for their turtleneck but they dunk and hide from me but this shell caught a body. So... please someone help me find my lost keys because this feeling ain't write from me!

Monday's Letter

Dear Spiritual Guide

I can feel your eyes lay on mine. So you know I see no lies. I knew this would happen in due time. So much pain I don't feel I can cry. Finally, I connected with a part of my demise. Now I gotta tear my son's eyes. Letting him know that he's been living some type of lie. But there are two sides. My pupil not knowing this family side, what a crime. My heart was wrapped in a vine, seven seconds to say goodbye. Serving time from God's sign, praying, and hoping for freedom will arrive. Sanitized from the hate that might've been applied, suicidal! Thoughts were running through my mind because mine weren't mine. That had my mind in a mine digging from a mine. Collapsing affects lifelines with a life on the line. I'm the one who saw calendars fly by waiting on father time to call time. But he will never see it from his optic as I will always be viewed from the side!

Monday's Letter

Dear Pale

The lack of color in your face when I saw the fear in your eyes. When the sky opened up I saw god delivered on time. The tears I saw in your cry over your crime in which you were so high. You saw burry lines in between the sidelines. Until the end of time, how could you become an angel of mine? When your love is declined with the transaction of a bond, that's how you end up with negative vibes. You owe tides. Not saying that you owe me but you held me at the ocean's feet. Leaving me at sea body flowing in the water as you tried to baptize me. God forgive me for any sin that I might seek in these letters as 26 cuts covered my body. Defacing the temple pregame ritual throwing up your ashes to show God has blessed you! God bless you without the tissue hanging out the organs that's what killed you. Irregular heartbeat John Q when I took over the hospital. How can you not see I went to the end of the world flat was never in my circle. So I leave you and always feel like, how could you?!

Monday's Letter

Dear Darkness

As I weather your storm waiting for a light
to turn on I continue to drift off. Waves raging,
from side to side making an emotional song. The
beat longs until nighttime falls while the melody
hums soft. The cries ring on that you can hear it
from the abyss's floor. With the audience
standing on the shore watching you drown while
wrapped around the cord. As it cuts life off, your
memory can live on. Or you can open your eyes
because you were born to be strong!

Monday's Letter

Dear Rain

I can feel you falling down my face. Into a place where the feeling seems to never change. Into a mood that is cold to the roots but beauty can always fill the room. The exact meaning of confused but your sleeves got you. People console you with that good book with words that are supposed to "uphold" you. Flowing in the riverbanks waiting to hit a mistake so it can overturn you. As you search for the old you everyone swears they know you but couldn't see that you didn't even know you! But how could this be possible, downpour overflowing the trenches, rags to riches but bags are missing. I mean BLACKS are missing. On a cold day ready for gunplay slap Envy for an apology on a space. Misty on a cloudy day dancing in pain because it's always a Lil Saint! Weather change might make me participate a chilly 50 always look good on my plate. It's never too late to look in the face of a great… I mean grapes, where spirits can interface and integrate into a body from a rental place. God can call for his body any day and, rainy days can call for happy paint.

Monday's Letter

Dear Wet Rule

The feeling of drops dripping down on me, my body reacts to the way my mind leaves. Leaves as fall got me on a bended knee. Winter froze up on me but my heart didn't get cold, I felt spring, spring on me. I can still smell Summer's Eve in the Summer's heat. Type of wetness where I couldn't breathe but to conceive the joy of what can come out of me. Change speeds, slow motion but it's looking like high speed when she running away from me. Caught too deep is the reason Y you have your feet above me like a palm tree. Unwind me, slow wine on me with that Georgia peach. Shorty probably has never been to a Georgia beach. Tap feet, so happy that you provided me with this big O feast. But who said I wanted you to ride me?! I just wanted to eat.

Monday's Letter

Dear Misunderstood

They want to crucify me to a Tee. Say, I'm too street. Man, that's all hood tendencies. Just because I don't talk like you and move like you. Paint a picture for your view. Come to my hood. Open the window, so you can get a bird's eye view. Of everyone doing what they do. Go to the tree, make the punch. How do you like rum? You can see the .45 tucked. Feeling like their in a gold rush. Or have the worst luck. Bag up, it's about to be the first of the month. Parked up, the Dz watching every day of the month. Suit up for the worst luck. They love to run down in the middle of the gold rush. Ice cup! They found the Hennessy trucked. Now run, they saw the tree punch. We do us. The bird's eye doesn't always represent us. Out the window, the hood is something I can't flush. With their view, they love painting their pictures of us. Move like you?! You see why I don't talk like you. See how the tendencies do. Too street, they wore tees when they finally crucified me. Outside thinking, inside of me.

Monday's Letter

Dear Art

Can they not see?! This right here is for me. Is my voice too strong to carry?! Or is it because I represent the streets? I feel like they are forgetting about me just because I can't identify a Michelangelo piece. Barely can quote Shakespeare, like I see thy window. But if I'm standing in front of a window is because the police think someone can ID me. Well, if I'm lucky enough to even make it that deep. I'm just trying to close the gap between what's real and what's facts. And at the same time, fight not to become a stat. Not to regress my level of being black. Damn right, we are always under attack. Why do you think I walk around with the attach-ment just in case I gotta clip a brother back? It is what it is. It's to be or not to be that smart hood brother trying to run from the street. Even though it continuously tries to jump me or be that street brother who falls in line with what was seen in the house and on TV. Corrupting my little mind why do you think people bug out for the coco, cherry, mango icy! It was every kid's dream. That's why I always said I'm chasing the green by any means. Daddy was there but he was high on the substance they were pitching in the streets. Leaving me to be who I knew I ain't

want to be. But I wanted to be that person
throwing that curve so it changed up on me. I
ruined a lot of people's family trees. Just like the
roots that were embedded in me. I guess they cut
the weed or better yet opportunities away from
me. I fell victim to the system and the stress.
Finally, I saw that no one was going to take
those open shots for me. Ghetto Gospel!

Monday's Letter

Dear Split

You can see they ain't who they say they are, Phoniness. Fake Gz, they were never really Gucci. I picked up the fake scent, that was stitched in their outfits, outlets! Handing out bullets like an outlet. Thank momma for your last fit, madness. More clips, keep shooting til you're open. Clinch fist, move it up like a stick shift. I won't miss all the drugs and the violence. High risk, they love to pay homage. Sell bricks til the fiends won't need their next fix. Momma's shift started with her tweaking for her next fixes. Rise this, and show praise to who you believe in. Believe this, you hood rich. Daddy couldn't see through the substance. Sentence, because his friend's pen started to tell their secrets. But peep this, this is just another street twist. The plot is thick, I pop this. The environment raises this. I rise fifth, cave in. The feelings of street sins. In a street sense, makes no sense why you love this. It made you feel hopeless like the first time the cord split. Now you a chorus! Record this! Statistics! The same day my eyes split! Wide open!

Monday's Letter

Dear Dream

I opened my eyes from a dream I just had. Where it's momma crying babies dying all over gun violence. Seeing the streets as the best opportunity to see heavy green. Doing it for the love of the cream because that's what's rule we. Too blind to see we are all blessed kings that are above these streets. No need to bring a piece just bring peace, PEACE! We can't live in immortality. The streets don't love me just hugs which brings light to our reality. Crack pipes, dime bags, oven bags, and friends getting zipped up or shipped up. This sh!t is messed up. But how am I'm not supposed to fall in love with the streets if everywhere I turn I'm in the belly of a beast?

What a dream! Back to sleep.

The government is trying to control us by feasting on our inability to see past the four blocks that we meet. Supplying the street forcing us to hold heat. No heat where we sleep or no food to eat. Momma was weak, Daddy, deadbeat! All odds against me. God can't help me, the school system, can't teach! Pay cuts for

the wealthy. PAIN cuts for the poor me. No
government funding back in OUR community.
Can't live Doctor King's dream if they still see
color instead of a heartbeat. My heart bleeds, it
hurts standing here selling the same stuff that
took my mom's from me. But I got to eat, my
parents were subject to the streets and I'm the
product of such reach. I can't sleep. This is no
dream, it's our his-tory. We can be all we can't
beat, the streets forever hold me. When I needed
a hug, it became my big homie.

Monday's Letter

Dear Unseen

I wish I could Ray Charles yesterday. Reset the heart, slide up like the Five Heartbeats catch a show, so something magic can come from me. I get lost in reality. When I touch this stage I don't feel anything but aggression coming from me with all this madness that surrounds me. You can see the heat from my pen, then y'all put a mic in front of me. I moved it to the side and watched it lean on me. Y'all can't picture my imagery. Wish I could control my demons off the string, long nose, it ain't Pippen nor Pinocchio. Stuff it up, that's how you sinus the Noes! Shh! I wish I could have unseen the sound with the bad zipped up with my brother in it like the coroner done fit it. And if I see God, I'm tee off with it! Yall can't tell me not to have a disagreement with the highest bidder, the cig is lit up, and he took my dog… IT'S A JOHN WICK PICTURE! I'm coming to get everyone who is responsible, it's per-son-al. Open my folder, y'all inside my per-son-al. These people don't like me like they know me in per-son-al. Talk sh!t behind my back like it's per-son-al. It's crazy because I see a couple of them in per-son-al! I'm so nice, I'll freestyle in the mind of my round. I did it in the book too, y'all know how I get in per-son-al!

You know how many times I can flip per-son-al,
split! I don't even know which person I am now.
But I'm a lost soul, I reach in the belt to grab a
.22 and have it sing for me. Wait! This is
supposed to be poetry, let me translate exactly
what I mean.

Dear Unseen

I wish I could say goodbye to yesterday. Reset a
heartbeat and catch a show so I can release to
pain from me. Wait! Did God come down and
break down that good book? I want to do the
same with my poetry. Since y'all like my energy,
y'all mind as well follow, I'm healthy I'm
gluten-free. And before y'all spit y'all peace,
thank God……. BECAUSE HE IS A
BROTHER LIKE ME! GHETTO GOSPEL!
BABII, ITS EAZY!!!

Monday's Letter

www.ingramcontent.com/pod-product-compliance
Lightning Source LLC
La Vergne TN
LVHW010850200726

843508LV00012B/2840